Inspired by the Word of God

Contents
Preface

Mary's Story

Connie's Reflection

Song List

His Love Endures
Jesus Spoke Softly To Me
The Kingdom Of God
There Is No Greater Love
God's Wonderful Grace
Search Me O God
God's Grace
Consider The Lilies
God Is Holy
No Greater Love
Lead Me In Truth
How Did You Spend Your Time?

Music and Words Composed by Mary Taylor ©2020

Preface

In 1966 I became a part of Fred and Arlene Davis' family from Camden. Arlene was a great pianist and singer for the Rockport Baptist church. The Davis's children sang and played instruments, and this exposure from my new extended family is where my love for music began. Arlene gave me piano lessons at that time and I was soon playing and rehearsing special music for church services. We often practiced after school and had fun. That year I began playing organ while she played piano at the church.

I have many fond memories of all the good times at the Davis home. I loved playing the old hymns. The first hymn I learned was "Wonderful Words Of Life". I feel it was a special gift from God to be able to play in church at such an early age. Soon I was playing organ one week and piano the next.

People started to approach me asking, "would you teach me?" After consideration I decided why not? So I started to teach others and felt such joy to see others learning and playing the piano.

Religious music is my favorite genre, the old Hymns are beautiful to sing and play. My favorite song is "Amazing Grace" because it reminds me of His Grace and how he came down from Heaven to save me from my sins and the promise of eternal life thereafter.

I have had other teachers who were also amazing musicians. All of my teachers taught me well. From them I learned classical, ragtime and blues. With this background, I sat down one day and wrote a melody, which led to chords, to lyrics and voila!, I had my first composition. This led to many other inspirational songs included in this book. It is a learning process and requires many hours. I am grateful to have had my friend and singer Connie Keep to interpret my compositions and bring them to musical life. My mother Mary Hodgkin's deserves credit for introducing me to the Holy Bible which she read to us kids all the time.

This book is my first endeavor and we enjoyed putting it together for you and hope you enjoy and are inspired by it, as I was inspired by dear and patient Arlene Davis.

In the future I am planning a children's book of songs.

Mary Taylor

Mary's Story

My interest in piano began before my teen years. I was influenced by listening and hearing Gospel songs played at our church. My first piano teacher was Arlene Davis who took me on as a student when I was 12 years old. After completing "Junior Hymn books 1 and 2 she had me playing four part harmony.

Another teacher I was blessed to have studied with was Glen Jenks, he taught me for three years, he loved to teach "rag time" music, his specialty.

I also studied under Carrie Landrith Clements, a very good pianist and Christian music player who passed a lot of her knowledge of Gospel songs to me. She taught me about theory and arrangement. She had many recitals, which were a lot of fun and helpful in my development.

Soon I began to play for the congregation at Rockport Baptist Church. It was a dream come true for me and I couldn't have done it without the support and inspiration from these fine musicians and God's gift to me as a pianist.

I love music and love inspiring others with my music. Several years ago I decided to write my own songs. I went to Bay Chamber Of Music School, and there I found another outstanding teacher named Mary Ann Driscoll. She helped me with some of my earlier compositions

I hope you enjoy these songs I have written. I intend on continuing writing and playing. It's been an interesting journey and I feel so blessed to be doing what I love and sharing with others.

Sincerely,

Mary Taylor

Connie's Reflection

What defines a person as a life is lived, and years pile up? More than careers, success, reputation, little remains in the summation of a life except what animates the soul and spirit. Mine was MUSIC. I remember my father repeating to me over and over:

"When you were a child, you could repeat any song you heard on the radio." This love of music and this ability to sing was God's gift to me, and I am so honored to share in Mary Taylor's composition of the many Christian hymns included in these CD's and translate her creativity into song. All of us have heard as we grew up that SONG is the truest expression of the soul and spirit....and certainly so much more is this true when singing music which honors the God whose life is shared by all living creatures, and so intimately by human beings. Lord, this is my gift to you. May it honor you and lead those who listen to Mary's compositions, to find a connection to that dynamic source which animates the universe, and at the center of the universe our own individual lives. Be blessed, all of you who can hear the pulse of His Love for each one of us.

Connie Keep

Psalms 18:1

The Lord is my rock and my deliver; My God, my strength, in who I will trust.

The Lord Is My Rock
Lead Sheet

Mary Taylor

rock and He is my sal va - tion

He is my sal - va - tion

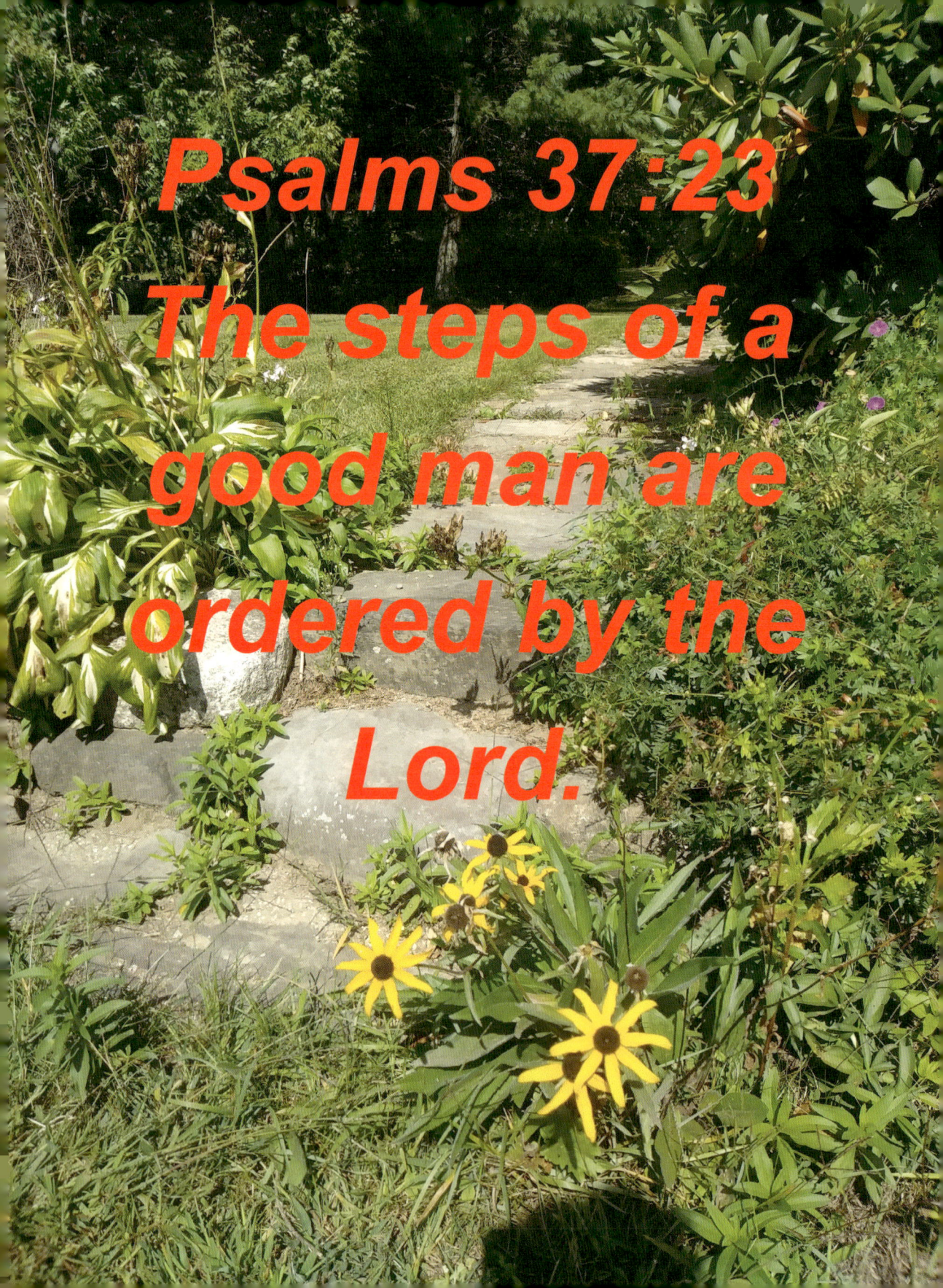

Psalms 37:23 The steps of a good man are ordered by the Lord.

Steps of A Good Man
Lead Sheet

Mary Taylor

1. The steps of
2. The steps of

a good man are or - dered by the Lord If he fall
a good man are or - dered by the Lord If he fall

He shall not be cast down the Lord will hold his hand

The steps of a good man are or -dered by the

Lord by the Lord the Lord

Ephesians 7:1

"He is so rich in kindness and grace that he purchased our freedom with the blood of his son and forgave our sins."

Calvary's Cross

Mary Taylor

Ephesians 7:1 "He is so rich in kindness and grace that he purchased
our freedom with the blood of his son and forgave our sins."
Music Words Composed by Mary Taylor

43

by   the   blood   of   the   lamb

John 15:13

There is no greater love than to lay his life for his friends.

I Will Lay Down My Life

Mary Taylor

John 15:13 There is no love greater love than to lay his life for his
friends. Music Words Composed by Mary Taylor © 2020

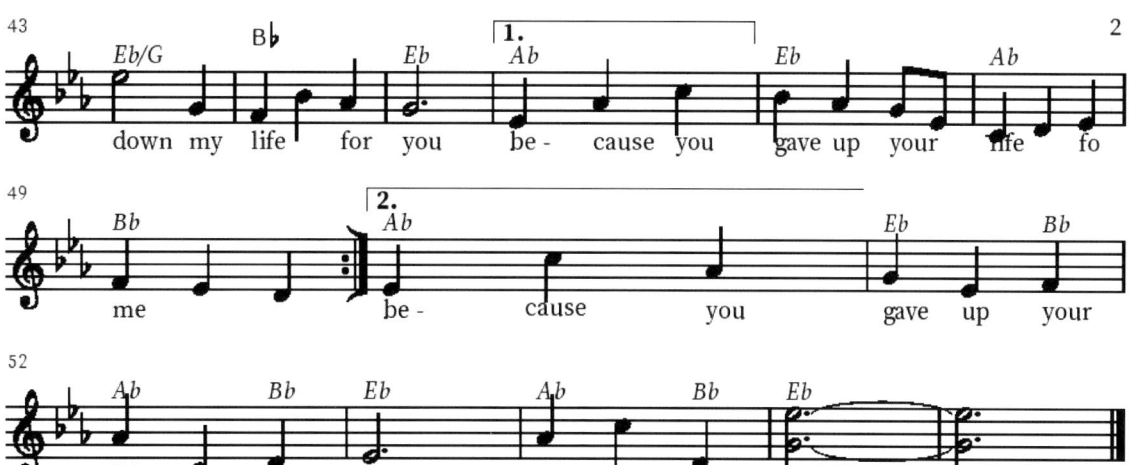

John 14:2

In my fathers house are many mansions if it were not so I would have told you so.

There's Heaven

Mary Taylor

Psalms 46:1

God is our refuge and strength, a very present help in trouble.

God Is My Refuge

Lead Sheet

Mary Taylor

Psalms 46:1 God is our refuge and strength. Music Words
Composed by Mary Taylor © 2020

Psalms 86:12

I will praise you, Lord my God, with all my heart, I will glorify your name forever.

I Will Praise You Lord

Lead Sheet

Mary Taylor

Refrain

I will praise you Lord with my whole heart

I will tell of your mar - ve - lous

work Yes I will Yes I will

I Peter 5:6

Anyone who does not love does not know God, because God is love.

God's Great Love
Lead Sheet

Mary Taylor

1. There is no love great-er then God's love
2. There is no love pur-er then God's love

It is a love that's deep-er then any sea   It's a love that's
It is a love so mer-ci-ful and full of grace

is so won-der-ful it's a love that's true   It's a love that's

so a-maz-ing a love so great   a love so great

Bridge

3. There is no love that's high-er then God's love   It is a love that's

so faith-ful and a-maz-ing   It's a love that

I Peter 6 Anyone who does not love does not know God, because
God is love. Music Words Composed by Mary Taylor © 2020

God's Command
Lead Sheet

Mary Taylor

John 13:34 A new commandment I give you love one another as
I have loved you. Music Words Composed by Mary Taylor © 2020

Acts 16:31

Believe on the Lord Jesus Christ and thou shall be saved.

Do You Want To Go To Heaven?
Lead Sheet

Mary Taylor

Acts 16:31 Believe on the Lord Jesus Christ and thou shall be saved
Music Words Composed by Mary Taylor © 2020

Psalms 27

The Lord is my light and my salvation; Whom shall I fear? The Lord is my strength of my life; of whom shall I be afraid?

The Lord Is My Light

Mary Taylor

Psalms 27 The Lord is my light and my salvation whom shall I fear Music Words Composed by Mary Taylor © 2020

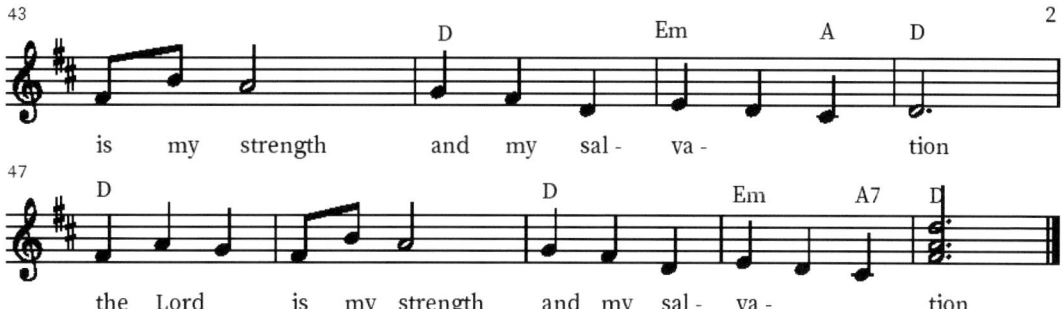

is my strength and my sal - va - tion

the Lord is my strength and my sal - va - tion

Psalms 147:1

Praise the Lord: For he is good to sing praises to our Lord.

He Is Worthy
Lead Sheet

Mary Taylor

1. When we come to God's house let's pra-ise his ho-ly
2. When we come to God's house let's pra-ise his ho-ly

name let's lift up our vo-ices to the Lord to pra-ise his
name let's lift up our vo-ices to the Lord to pra-ise our

Refrain

name Sing to the Lord bless his name for he is good
King

Sing to the Lord and re-joice for he is wor-thy to be praised

wor-thy to be praised

Bridge

3. We thank you Lord

for this day we will praise you We thank you Lord

Psalms 147:1 Praise the Lord for he is good to sing praises to our Lord
Music Words Composed by Mary Taylor © 2020

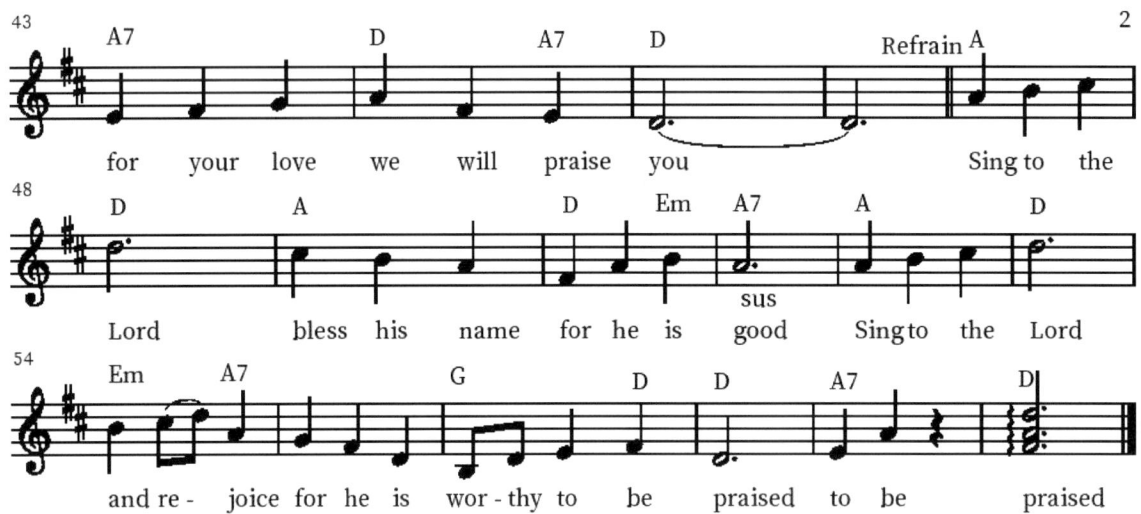

God's Creation

Notes

Notes

Notes

Notes